LUCIANO MONARDEZ

Dad, Driver, Provider

Navigating Rideshare Work and Family

Contents

Introduction

Why Drive?

Hey there, welcome! If you're here, you're likely a dad looking for a better way to balance work and family. Maybe you're already driving or considering jumping in—either way, I'm glad you're here.

Let's get right to it: I have been a gig worker for over 13 years. I can't begin to express how it changed my life. Long story short, 14 years ago I had a devastating year and a half. I got divorced, lost my Dad, had a heart attack, and lost my job. I was having trouble finding a job, and quite honestly had a lot of stress about working in an office again with other people. So you can say I originally fell into this out of necessity, but I'm glad I decided to try it. It ended up being exactly what I needed to rebuild my life.

Gig work offers something you won't often find in a 9-to-5—*freedom*. Imagine a schedule that revolves not around a boss but your kids' soccer games, family dinners, and school drop-offs. I for one can say I am glad I was there for that. As a rideshare driver, *you're the one in control*. You choose when to work and when to be home. This flexibility can be a game-changer for dads like us. There's no corporate ladder, no office politics. The pride and independence that come from this kind of work can't be overstated. In the gig world, *you're in charge*, and that's an incredible feeling.

Now, let's tackle the big question: *Can you make real money doing this?* Yes, you can. With the right strategy, you can make a solid income— even enough to support your family full-time. It's not about getting rich overnight, but about building a sustainable path to support your loved ones, *your way.*

And here's the best part: you are your own boss.

In the pages ahead, I'll guide you through everything you need to go from curious to confident—from understanding peak hours to finding balance with family time. This isn't just about driving; it's about carving out a life that lets you be a provider *and* a present dad. So, buckle up, and let's get going!

1

Starting Strong - Setting Up for Success

Essential Preparations for Your First Rideshare Shift

A lright, so you're ready to hit the road. Before you dive into your first shift, let's make sure you've got the essentials covered. Driving for rideshare isn't just about picking up passengers—it's about setting yourself up to work smarter, keep your car in top shape, and have a clear financial plan. Getting these basics down will save you a lot of stress later and help you maximize your earnings right from the start.

1. The Right Tools and Apps for the Job

Efficiency is everything in the rideshare game, and a few key tools can make all the difference. First up, you'll need your rideshare platform's app (Uber, Lyft, or whichever one you're driving for). But don't stop there—grab a few others to streamline your shift. A good navigation app like Google Maps or Waze is essential to find the best routes and avoid traffic. And consider a mileage-tracking app (Stride or Everlance, for example) to keep tabs on your mileage for tax purposes.

Some drivers also find apps like GasBuddy helpful to save on fuel, and customer-service apps to manage ratings and feedback. The more you simplify your tools, the more you'll be able to focus on what matters: making money and getting your passengers safely from A to B.

2. Car Maintenance and Insurance Essentials

Your car is your moneymaker, so keeping it in top shape is non-negotiable. Start with regular maintenance—oil changes, tire rotations, and routine checks. Not only will this help avoid breakdowns, but it can also improve fuel efficiency, saving you money in the long run. Frequent tire rotations extend the life of your tires as well. Keep a cleaning kit in the car to make sure the interior is always passenger-ready. First impressions matter, and a clean car can make a positive impact on ratings(and tips).

Insurance is another big one. Check that your personal insurance covers rideshare driving, or look into rideshare-specific policies to protect yourself. Most platforms offer limited insurance when you're on a trip, but having your own coverage fills in the gaps. Knowing you're fully covered gives you peace of mind, so you can focus on the road.

3. Financial Planning Basics and Goal-Setting

Rideshare driving can be an income boost, or a full-time gig if you play it right. But either way, having a financial plan is key to making this work for your family. Set a weekly or monthly income goal and break it down by the number of hours or shifts you need to hit that target. Having a clear plan keeps you from overworking and lets you find a balance with family time.

Next, set aside funds for expenses—gas, maintenance, and even taxes, since you're likely working as an independent contractor. A little planning goes a long way. Also, consider an emergency fund to cover any unexpected expenses or slow weeks.

With these essentials in place, you're ready to start strong. Being prepared means less stress, more earnings, and a smoother journey on your rideshare path.

Understanding Your Market and Peak Hours

Driving for rideshare isn't just about cruising around and waiting for rides. To make serious income, you've got to know your market and make the most of peak hours. This section will show you how to identify high-demand areas, leverage peak times, and maximize your earnings each hour you're on the road.

1. Identifying High-Demand Areas in Your City

Every city has its own unique flow. There are certain neighborhoods, shopping districts, event venues, and airport areas that attract a lot of riders. Spend some time getting to know the high-demand zones where you're likely to get consistent requests. Start with popular areas like downtown, business districts, and busy nightlife spots—these tend to have a steady stream of passengers, especially during peak times.

Events are another big opportunity. Sports games, concerts, and festivals create huge demand spikes, so it's worth knowing the major event schedules in your area. If you're in a city with a large university, keeping an eye on the academic calendar can also help you anticipate times when more students and visitors might need rides.

2. How Peak Hours Affect Your Income

Peak hours are prime time for rideshare drivers. These hours, typically in the early morning (commuter hours), evening rush hour, and late-night weekends, are when demand is highest—and platforms often increase fares to encourage more drivers to get on the road. Driving during these hours can significantly boost your earnings with less waiting time between rides.

Familiarize yourself with the peak hours specific to your market. For example, commuter-heavy cities might see more early-morning requests, while college towns might have late-night demand on weekends. By timing your shifts to align with peak hours, you can maximize your trips and reduce downtime, leading to higher income per shift.

3. Strategies for Maximizing Earnings Per Hour

Maximizing earnings isn't just about working longer; it's about working smarter. Start by planning your shifts around those peak hours and high-demand areas. Sticking to high-traffic zones increases your chances of back-to-back rides, reducing idle time.

Additionally, use bonuses or incentives offered by the platform. Many rideshare apps provide bonuses for completing a certain number of rides within a specific time or staying in high-demand areas. These incentives can give your earnings a nice boost if you plan them right.

Finally, keep an eye on surge pricing. When demand outstrips supply, platforms raise prices, which means more money for you. This often happens during peak times, bad weather, or large events. If you can be in a surge zone when it happens, you can earn significantly more per ride.

With these strategies, you'll know where to be, when to drive, and how to make the most of each shift. The road to higher earnings starts with understanding your market, so take the time to learn it—and watch your income grow.

Creating a Balanced Schedule from Day One

One of the biggest advantages of rideshare driving is the ability to create your own schedule. But without clear priorities, it's easy to get pulled into driving too much or too little, losing out on income or family time. By planning a balanced schedule from the start, you'll set yourself up to succeed both as a driver and as a dad.

1. Block Out Family Commitments First

Start by listing all your family commitments each week—school drop-offs, bedtime routines, family meals, sports practices, and other activities you don't want to miss. Blocking these out in your calendar *first* makes it easier to build your driving shifts around what matters most. Once those family times are protected, you can look at your available hours for driving.

Then, map out your open time slots. Maybe mornings are ideal for driving after school drop-offs, or evenings work better if your mornings are busier. Structuring your schedule this way lets you maximize your hours on the road without missing key family moments.

Action Steps:

- List your weekly family commitments, add them to your calendar, and mark them as unavailable.
- Find open time slots where driving can fit around family life.

2. Leverage Flexible Hours to Earn More Efficiently

The great thing about rideshare driving is that your hours can be flexible—so make them work for you! If your schedule allows, try different shift patterns (such as a couple of shorter shifts instead of one long one) to see what keeps you energized and productive.

Look at your local peak times for rides, like morning and evening rush hours or weekends. By driving during peak demand, you're able to maximize earnings in less time. For instance, an hour during peak times can be worth two off-peak hours in terms of income. If you focus your shifts around these periods, you'll make the most out of your available time.

Action Steps:

- Experiment with different shift patterns to see which are most effective for your schedule and energy.
- Drive during peak demand hours for the best earnings per hour.

3. Set Work Limits to Avoid Burnout

With the flexibility of gig work, it's easy to keep picking up rides. But without limits, burnout can creep up fast, affecting both your health and time with your family. Decide in advance on a realistic number of weekly hours based on your income goals, and then break those down into manageable daily shifts. This way, you know when you're on track, and it's easier to stop when you hit your target.

Also, plan for rest days each week. Just as with a traditional job, taking time off helps you recharge, stay motivated, and keep family time a priority. Stick to these limits, and you'll be able to sustain a strong balance between work and home.

Action Steps:

- Set a weekly goal for driving hours based on your income needs, and break it down by day.
- Schedule one or two rest days each week to keep burnout at bay.

With this approach, you'll establish a schedule that lets you earn reliably *and* be there for your family. By blocking out family commitments, using peak hours, and setting realistic limits, you're creating a plan that's both effective and balanced from day one.

2

Effective Strategies for Growth

Optimizing Routes and Minimizing Downtime

W hen it comes to rideshare driving, knowing the best routes and minimizing downtime are essential for maximizing earnings. This section will cover practical navigation tips, using real-time data to avoid traffic, and strategies for reducing gaps between rides. Let's get into how you can keep the wheels turning and make the most of every shift.

1. Learning Navigation Tips and Tricks

Getting familiar with your city's layout is a game-changer in rideshare driving. While GPS apps like Google Maps or Waze are your best friends, local knowledge helps you adapt when these tools fall short. Start by learning the main routes to popular areas, like airports, downtown, and major attractions.

Familiarity with alternative routes lets you adjust on the fly if there's sudden traffic or a road closure.

Another useful tip is to zoom out on your GPS app occasionally. This view gives you a big-picture look at nearby routes and possible traffic issues, helping you make better decisions about the fastest way to reach a destination.

Action Steps:

- Spend time getting to know major routes and backroads in your area.
- Use the GPS's zoom-out feature to spot traffic patterns and nearby routes.

2. Utilizing Real-Time Data to Avoid Traffic

Traffic is one of the biggest obstacles to quick, efficient rides, so using real-time data to avoid it can make a significant difference in your earnings. Apps like Waze and Google Maps provide live traffic information, alerting you to congestion, roadblocks, or accidents. Make a habit of checking traffic conditions before and during your shift, especially if you're driving during rush hours.

Some apps even show real-time locations of other drivers, which helps you avoid overly crowded areas and head toward places where you're more likely to get a ride request.

Action Steps:

- Use apps like Google Maps or Waze for live traffic updates.
- Regularly check traffic conditions and adjust your route if needed.

3. Reducing Gaps Between Rides

Reducing downtime between rides is key to maximizing your hourly earnings. The best way to do this is to position yourself in high-demand areas. After a drop-off, don't just stay put—take a minute to check nearby demand zones. Airports, busy shopping districts, and event venues are usually good spots. Some rideshare apps even show "hot zones" with high demand, so be sure to keep an eye on these areas.

If you're wrapping up a ride in a quieter part of town, consider heading back toward a high-traffic area while you wait for your next request. Driving toward popular zones keeps you active rather than idling, which can reduce the time between rides and make each shift more productive.

Action Steps:

- After each ride, position yourself closer to high-demand areas.
- Check your app's "hot zones" or demand areas to minimize idle time.

By mastering navigation, avoiding traffic, and minimizing downtime, you can work smarter, not harder. With these tactics, you'll keep your shifts efficient and your earnings steady.

Handling Rideshare App Promotions and Bonuses

Another great advantage of working with rideshare apps is the variety of bonuses and promotions they offer to boost your earnings. Knowing how to evaluate and strategically use these incentives can make a big difference in hitting your income targets. Let's dive into how you can make the most of promotions, strategize for higher earnings, and balance multiple apps for maximum profit.

1. How to Evaluate and Capitalize on Bonuses

Rideshare apps often run promotions like "complete X number of rides for an extra $Y" or "drive during peak hours to earn a bonus." It can be tempting to go for every promotion, but not all bonuses are equally profitable. Before you commit, evaluate whether the terms align with your schedule and are worth the effort.

For instance, if a bonus requires a high number of rides in a limited time, but only during off-peak hours, it may not be worth sacrificing time that could be spent in higher-paying zones. On the other hand, bonuses that coincide with peak hours or locations you frequently drive in can be easy to achieve with minimal changes to your routine.

Action Steps:

- Review the terms of each promotion and compare them to your current schedule.
- Prioritize bonuses that align with peak times or areas with high demand for better efficiency.

2. Strategic Acceptance to Reach Earning Targets

Many bonuses require completing a set number of rides within a specific period. To make the most of these, plan your shifts to hit the ride target without overextending yourself. This might mean taking shorter, high-frequency trips during peak hours, which lets you hit your ride goal faster and helps you avoid burnout from long drives.

If the bonus requires back-to-back rides, avoid declining too many requests, as it could slow down your momentum. Accepting rides strategically—based on distance, location, and time of day—can help you reach your target without exhausting yourself.

Action Steps:

- Plan shifts to include more short trips if the bonus is ride-count based.
- Focus on high-frequency areas to reach the ride target quickly and efficiently.

3. Managing Promotions Across Multiple Apps

If you're working with multiple rideshare apps (e.g., Uber, Lyft), you'll likely encounter overlapping promotions. Managing promotions across apps takes a bit of juggling, but it can significantly boost your overall income. Start by checking each app's bonus offers at the start of your shift, and choose which ones are easiest to complete based on your schedule and goals.

For example, if one app has a high-value bonus for completing rides during peak hours and another has a less rewarding promotion, focus on the one with higher returns. Switch between apps based on which promotions are available and prioritize those that align with your target income. Many drivers find that splitting shifts or alternating apps by day lets them maximize promotions without feeling stretched thin.

Action Steps:

- Compare bonus offers on each app at the start of each shift.
- Focus on the app with the highest-earning potential and switch when appropriate.

By carefully evaluating bonuses, accepting rides strategically, and balancing multiple apps, you can optimize your shifts for higher earnings with less effort. Promotions and bonuses are valuable tools—use them wisely, and you'll see your income grow.

Maximizing Tips and Customer Satisfaction

Providing a great experience for riders is key to building steady tips, maintaining high ratings, and enjoying a smoother rideshare career. With just a few thoughtful actions, you can make a strong impression on riders, increase your income, and improve your standing on the platform. Here are some practical tips for enhancing the customer experience, using reviews to your advantage, and handling difficult customers with professionalism.

1. Simple Ways to Enhance Customer Experience

A good experience often starts with a clean and comfortable ride. Keeping your car tidy shows riders you're invested in their comfort and in providing a pleasant environment. This can be as simple as giving your car a quick once-over before each shift, wiping down surfaces, and keeping it free of clutter.

Small touches make a big difference, too. If it's within your budget, offering basic amenities like bottled water, phone chargers, or a choice of music can go a long way. Greet each passenger warmly, ask them if they have a preferred route, and respect their preferences—some might want to chat, while others might prefer a quiet ride.

Action Steps:

- Start each shift with a clean, fresh car to make a good first impression.
- Consider offering small extras like water, phone chargers, or choice of music.

- Respect riders' preferences for conversation or quiet and adjust the temperature if they request it.

2. Understanding the Power of Reviews

In the rideshare world, reviews are more than just numbers—they're your reputation. High ratings improve your visibility in the app, can qualify you for higher earnings or special bonuses, and even make riders more comfortable choosing you. Encouraging good reviews doesn't have to be awkward; a simple comment like, "Thanks for riding with me—feedback is always appreciated!" at the end of a trip can nudge satisfied passengers to leave positive feedback.

Be proactive with reviews. Take time each week to look at recent feedback for patterns. Are passengers mentioning your friendliness, or are they asking for a smoother ride? Regularly incorporating feedback helps you keep improving, leading to higher ratings and, often, better tips.

Action Steps:

- End trips on a positive note, politely reminding riders that feedback is welcome.
- Review your feedback regularly to spot trends and see where you can improve.

3. Handling Difficult Customers Professionally

Every rideshare driver will encounter difficult passengers now and then. The key is to handle these situations calmly and professionally, as these moments can impact both your mood and ratings. For riders who seem frustrated or critical, stay polite and keep your responses brief and neutral. If a customer makes a difficult request or behaves inappropriately, calmly set boundaries—your priority is safety and professionalism.

In cases where a situation becomes unsafe or highly uncomfortable, you have the option to end the ride. Most apps provide support for drivers in such cases, so don't hesitate to document any incidents and report them if necessary. Your ratings and feedback can benefit from professional handling of difficult situations, and these precautions help keep your experience positive, too.

Action Steps:

- Practice staying calm and neutral to manage challenging riders without escalating the situation.
- If a rider is disrespectful or unsafe, consider ending the ride and documenting the incident with the app's support tools.

With these strategies, you'll be well-equipped to increase tips, maintain high ratings, and handle challenging interactions professionally. By consistently focusing on customer satisfaction, you'll build a reputation that keeps riders happy and boosts your earnings.

3

Leveraging Multiple Streams for Higher Earnings

Multi-App Strategy and Switching Smartly

U sing multiple rideshare apps can be a powerful way to maximize your earnings, especially during peak hours and surge pricing events. However, managing multiple platforms effectively requires some planning and smart strategies to avoid conflicts. This section covers the best practices for juggling more than one app, managing surge pricing across platforms, and avoiding penalties or conflicts.

1. Best Practices for Using More Than One Rideshare App

Running more than one rideshare app can increase your chances of getting consistent rides and help you make the most of your time on the road. Start by installing the apps you plan to use, such as Uber, Lyft, or any others popular in your area. Then, get familiar with the unique features each app offers, as well as the areas where they tend to be busiest.

To balance multiple apps, try alternating between them based on demand patterns you notice. For example, if you're near a busy downtown area, you may find that one app consistently has higher demand there. By toggling back and forth, you'll increase your chances of landing rides quickly, especially during slow times on one platform.

Action Steps:

- Download and set up multiple apps, learning each platform's busy areas and peak times.
- Experiment with toggling between apps based on demand and location to find the best balance.

2. Managing Surge Pricing Across Platforms

Surge pricing (or "Prime Time" on some platforms) is when fares temporarily increase due to high demand. Running multiple apps during these periods can help you make the most of surge pricing opportunities, as each platform may have slightly different surge areas and times. When you see a surge on one app, switch to check if the other app is also experiencing increased rates.

If one app offers a better surge rate, prioritize it, but keep the other open for quick switching if the demand shifts. To stay efficient, avoid driving far out of your way to chase surges, as this can waste gas and time. Instead, focus on nearby surges that align with your current location.

Action Steps:

- Monitor both apps for surge pricing and prioritize the one with the highest rate.
- Stay within a reasonable radius when chasing surges to avoid excessive driving.

3. Avoiding App Conflicts and Penalties

While it's tempting to keep both apps active simultaneously, you'll need to be careful to avoid penalties or conflicts. Accepting a ride on one app while still showing availability on the other can lead to overlapping requests or even penalties. To prevent this, disable availability on the secondary app as soon as you accept a ride on your primary app.

Some drivers use app "switchers" or widgets that let them toggle availability quickly, making it easier to avoid accidental overlap. Additionally, watch out for policies that penalize drivers for frequent cancellations. If you accidentally accept a ride on both apps, complete the first ride and, if possible, inform the passenger on the other platform of a slight delay or cancel if absolutely necessary.

Action Steps:

- Disable the other app's availability immediately after accepting a ride to avoid overlap.
- Use app switchers or quick-access widgets to manage availability smoothly.
- Review each app's cancellation policies to avoid unnecessary penalties.

By following these multi-app strategies, you can balance multiple platforms for increased earnings without the hassle of conflicts or penalties. With smart toggling, efficient surge pricing management, and careful app handling, you'll be set up for success with a multi-app strategy that makes the most of each shift.

Exploring Complementary Gig Opportunities

Diversifying your gig work can provide additional income streams and add flexibility to your schedule. Beyond rideshare driving, options like food delivery and package transport can complement your primary gig and help smooth out earnings during low-demand hours. Here's how to explore these complementary gigs, when and how to incorporate them, and how to ensure they positively impact your overall income.

1. Options like Food Delivery and Package Transport

Food delivery services (like DoorDash, Uber Eats, and Grubhub) and package delivery platforms (such as Amazon Flex) are popular gig options that align well with rideshare driving. These services often have peak hours outside of traditional rideshare rush times, such as lunch and late-night hours for food delivery, or early mornings and afternoons for package delivery. By adding one or two of these services to your portfolio, you can increase your earning potential without necessarily overlapping your rideshare hours.

Delivering food or packages can also be less stressful than transporting passengers, especially on slower days or when you're looking for a change of pace. It's worth signing up for one or two complementary apps, testing out their workflows, and seeing which works best with your rideshare schedule.

Action Steps:

- Research local demand for food and package delivery services, and choose 1–2 apps to try.
- Consider food delivery for lunch and dinner rushes, and package delivery for mornings or afternoons.

2. When and How to Incorporate Additional Gigs

The key to successful gig stacking is timing. Try working on these other gigs during rideshare lulls or on days you prefer a mix of work. For instance, if you notice slow periods in your usual rideshare hours, you could switch to food delivery to stay active and keep your earnings consistent.

Another approach is to assign certain days or shifts to your secondary gigs. If weekends are busy for rideshare but weekdays are slower, consider dedicating a weekday to package deliveries or food runs. Just keep an eye on your schedule to avoid overcommitting, which can lead to burnout.

Action Steps:

- · Identify slow times in your rideshare schedule where adding a secondary gig could be beneficial.
- · Experiment with assigning specific days or shifts to complementary gigs to see how it impacts your weekly income.

3. Calculating the Impact on Your Primary Rideshare Income

Adding additional gigs can be profitable, but it's essential to keep track of how they affect your primary rideshare income. Track your earnings and hours spent on each gig separately, noting any changes in your overall take-home pay and hourly rate. The goal is to see if the additional gigs boost your income without significantly cutting into your rideshare profits or family time.

You might find that your total earnings increase during low-demand hours for rideshare driving, or you may discover that one type of gig is more efficient or enjoyable than another. By keeping track of these numbers, you can make informed decisions on how to structure your work week.

Action Steps:

- Track your income and hours for each gig separately and calculate your hourly earnings for both.
- Evaluate periodically to see if the additional gigs are enhancing or detracting from your primary rideshare income.

By exploring complementary gigs, you'll be able to increase your income potential while staying flexible and adapting to demand patterns. With careful planning and a smart approach to gig stacking, you can create a well-rounded strategy that keeps your income flowing and adds variety to your work.

Setting Monthly Income Goals and Tracking Progress

As a rideshare driver and gig worker, having clear income goals helps keep you on track and motivated. Setting and adjusting monthly targets, using reliable tracking tools, and identifying patterns in your work can all help you maximize your earnings and stay focused. Here's a guide to establishing income goals, tracking your progress, and spotting trends to boost your monthly income.

1. How to Set and Adjust Monthly Income Targets

Start by determining your essential financial needs—things like rent, bills, groceries, and any other fixed costs. Add a buffer for unexpected expenses, then set your income goal slightly above this total to give yourself room for savings or additional costs. Once you have your target, break it down into weekly and daily goals. For example, if you're aiming to make $5,000 a month, you'll need to average around $1,250 per week or $180 per day.

Don't hesitate to adjust your goals based on real-world experience. If you notice you're consistently hitting your daily targets with extra hours to spare, consider raising your goal. Or, if one month's demand is lower than expected, adjust to avoid burnout while staying within a comfortable earning range.

Action Steps:

- Calculate your monthly income goal based on essential expenses and financial goals.
- Break it down into manageable weekly and daily targets.
- Reevaluate your goal each month to ensure it's realistic and achievable.

2. Tools and Apps for Income Tracking

Keeping track of your income accurately is key to knowing where you stand in relation to your monthly goals. There are many tools and apps specifically designed for gig workers to track income, expenses, mileage, and more. Apps like Stride, Gridwise, and Everlance allow you to log earnings per shift, monitor expenses, and see an overview of your income trends.

Use these tools to input your daily earnings and shifts worked, and track other expenses like gas and maintenance. Consistently recording this data helps you see where your money is going and can reveal areas for improvement. Plus, these records are invaluable come tax season!

Action Steps:

- Download a gig-tracking app (like Stride, Gridwise, or Everlance) to log your income and expenses.
- Make a habit of inputting your earnings after each shift or at the end of each day for accuracy.
- Regularly review your tracked income to see how it compares to your goals.

3. Identifying Patterns and Trends to Boost Earnings

Over time, your tracking data can reveal useful insights, like peak earning times, high-demand areas, and your most productive hours. For example, you might notice that Thursday and Friday evenings yield higher earnings than other days, or that certain neighborhoods have consistent demand. Use these patterns to refine your schedule for maximum profitability.

Additionally, watching for seasonal trends can help you anticipate slow or busy periods. If you know that certain holidays or local events increase demand, you can plan your shifts accordingly. By adapting your schedule based on this data, you can increase your chances of reaching your income goals more efficiently.

Action Steps:

- Analyze your tracking data each month to spot trends in peak hours, busy areas, and seasonal patterns.
- Adjust your schedule to take advantage of high-demand periods and locations.
- Track changes in income after adjustments to see if they positively impact your earnings.

By setting clear monthly goals, using tracking tools, and adjusting your schedule based on trends, you can optimize your earnings with confidence. Keeping tabs on your income and expenses ensures that you stay on top of your goals and make the most of each shift.

4

Balancing Work and Family Life

Creating a Sustainable, Family-Friendly Schedule

Not to sound like a broken record, but one of the best parts of gig work is the flexibility it offers—but without structure, that flexibility can easily turn into a chaotic, unpredictable schedule. By creating a consistent, family-friendly routine, you can achieve the stability you need to reach your income goals while being there for your family. Here's how to build a sustainable schedule that supports both your work and family life.

1. Using Consistent Hours for Stability

A steady routine is key to maintaining both income and a sense of balance. Identify which hours work best for you and your family, considering when demand is highest in your area. For example, morning rush hours or evening commutes are often profitable times for rideshare, while lunchtime or late-night hours may work well for other gigs like food delivery.

Aim to set consistent hours each week. This can be as simple as dedicating certain blocks of time to work each day and sticking to them as closely as possible. By doing this, you'll know when you're available for work and when you're free to focus on family, creating a rhythm that's sustainable over the long term.

Action Steps:

- Identify the most profitable times in your area and set regular shifts around them.
- Create a consistent weekly schedule and communicate it with your family.
- Stick to your chosen hours as much as possible to keep work predictable.

2. How to Adjust for School Events, Vacations, etc.

Life happens, and as a parent, there are events you don't want to miss. With gig work, you can adapt your schedule to accommodate important family moments—school events, vacations, doctor's appointments, and more. Plan your work hours around these commitments by checking the family calendar each week and blocking off time in advance for anything non-negotiable.

If an unexpected event comes up, take advantage of your flexibility. Use slow hours or shifts with lower demand to make up for any missed time. Adjusting your work around family needs not only keeps you engaged in family life but also makes it easier for your family to support your work. This ability to show up to those events, but know you can still provide is such a boost to your confidence and a stress reliever.

Action Steps:

- Review the family calendar weekly to schedule around important events.
- Use slower work periods to make up for any lost hours when unexpected events arise.
- Build a system for adjusting your schedule that prioritizes both family and work needs.

3. Building Family Support and Understanding Around Your Schedule

Creating a family-friendly schedule requires communication and understanding. Share your work goals with your family so they understand the hours you've committed to and how these contribute to the family's finances and well-being. Let them know when you'll be available and explain the importance of sticking to your hours as part of your earning plan.

Encouraging family support can also mean inviting them to help you stay accountable, or involving them in planning fun family activities during your off hours. With a shared understanding, your family is more likely to support your routine, making it easier for you to maintain your schedule over time.

Action Steps:

- Share your work goals and schedule with your family so they understand your commitments.
- Invite your family to help plan activities during your off-hours to encourage balance.
- Establish a routine together that supports your work hours and family time.

By setting consistent hours, adjusting for family events, and communicating openly with your family, you'll be able to create a routine that supports both your work and family life. A well-planned schedule will not only help you achieve your income goals but also allow you to be present for the moments that matter most.

Managing Income Variability with Family Budgeting

One of the challenges of gig work is the natural variability in income. Some months may bring in more than enough, while others may fall short. By creating a proactive family budget, setting aside funds for lean months, and having open discussions about finances, you can build a system that brings stability to your household, even with an unpredictable income, and unexpected expenses.

1. Planning for Fluctuations in Monthly Earnings

The first step to managing income variability is to establish a family budget that accounts for both higher and lower earning months. Start by calculating your average monthly expenses—housing, utilities, groceries, and any other essential costs. Then, identify your baseline income: the minimum you need to cover these expenses each month. When you have a month where earnings exceed this amount, put any extra into a reserve fund to create a cushion for months that might fall short.

Consider building flexibility into your budget by categorizing expenses as "essential" and "non-essential." This way, if earnings dip one month, you can pause or reduce non-essential spending to stay on track financially without sacrificing the essentials. This will be most important at the beginning of your journey when you are in the investigation step. While you develope strategies for the best areas, times, and most profitable apps to use, you will be earning less than usual as you try different approaches. But remember you can always work more hours to make your goal for the day.

Action Steps:

- Calculate your baseline monthly income to cover essential expenses.
- Use higher-income months to build a reserve fund for leaner times.
- Categorize your family budget into essential and non-essential expenses to build flexibility.

2. Using a Reserve Fund for Leaner Months

A reserve fund is your safety net during slow months or unexpected expenses. Aim to build this fund gradually by setting aside a portion of your income every time you exceed your baseline goal. Ideally, try to save enough to cover at least one month's essential expenses. This buffer will allow you to navigate months with fewer rides or lower demand without worrying about covering bills.

When your income exceeds expectations, transfer a percentage to the reserve fund right away. Treat it as an essential expense, so the reserve becomes part of your overall financial plan. Using this approach, you'll be able to smooth out the ups and downs in income over time.

Action Steps:

- Build a reserve fund with a goal of covering one month's essential expenses.
- Contribute to the reserve whenever your income exceeds your monthly baseline.
- View the reserve fund as an essential part of your budget, tapping into it only when needed.

3. Discussing Finances with Your Family Effectively

Financial stability is a family effort, so it's crucial to talk openly about budgeting and income variability with your loved ones. Set aside time each month to review finances together, discuss the budget, and plan for any adjustments based on anticipated income. This keeps everyone on the same page and helps family members understand why sticking to the budget is important.

Explain how gig work income can fluctuate, and share your plan for managing these shifts. Involving your family in these discussions can also encourage them to support your budgeting efforts. If you're a single father, consider discussing financial priorities in an age-appropriate way to build a team mindset around your family's financial health.

Action Steps:

- Schedule monthly check-ins with your family to review finances and budget goals.
- Explain income variability and the purpose of a reserve fund so everyone understands the plan.
- Foster a supportive, team-based approach to budgeting and adjusting expenses as needed.

By planning for fluctuations, establishing a reserve fund, and openly discussing finances with your family, you can bring stability to your household, regardless of changes in monthly income. With a proactive budget in place, you'll be better prepared to handle the ups and downs of gig work with confidence and peace of mind.

Protecting Your Health and Well-Being

Now, rideshare work has its perks, but spending long hours on the road can take a toll on your body and mind if you're not careful. I fell into this trap and it's not fun. Prioritizing your physical health, building mental resilience, and planning for long-term sustainability are essential to staying productive and happy in your work. The feeling that continuing to work means continuing to earn is very tempting but can be very dangerous. Both to your health, and ability to drive safely. Here's how to create habits that protect your health and prevent burnout.

1. Maintaining Physical Health While Driving

Sitting for hours each day can lead to back pain, stiffness, and general discomfort. Combat this by incorporating simple stretches and movement breaks into your day. Aim to stop every hour or so, even if just for a few minutes, to get out of the car, stretch, and walk around. Regular movement helps improve circulation, reduces stiffness, and keeps you feeling alert.

Investing in ergonomically supportive equipment, like a seat cushion or lumbar support, can make a big difference as well. Make sure your seat is adjusted for comfort, with your back straight and your arms relaxed at the wheel. Staying hydrated and keeping healthy snacks on hand also help maintain your energy throughout the day. Remember to counter dehydrating drinks like coffee or energy drinks with water or electrolytes. Just because you are sitting doesn't mean you cant dehydrate, and that can cause mental fatigue.

Action Steps:

- Take a short movement break every hour to stretch and relieve stiffness. A short exercise session during your shift is not a bad idea.
- Use ergonomic accessories, like a seat cushion, to support good posture.
- Keep water and healthy snacks in the car to maintain energy and hydration.

2. Mental Strategies for Preventing Stress

The gig economy has its ups and downs, and handling those fluctuations without getting overwhelmed is key to mental well-being. Practice focusing on what you can control—like choosing high-demand times to work and planning breaks— while accepting that some factors, like traffic and customer behavior, are outside your control.

Consider practicing mindfulness techniques, like deep breathing or brief meditation exercises, to help reset your mind during stressful moments. Using positive self-talk and visualizing your goals can also keep you focused and optimistic, even when the workday is tough.

Action Steps:

- Set aside time for short mindfulness breaks, such as deep breathing or visualization, during the day.
- Focus on what you can control, like your schedule and attitude, while letting go of external stressors.
- Use positive self-talk to boost resilience and stay focused

on your goals.

3. Long-Term Planning to Avoid Burnout

To sustain this work over the long term, you'll need a plan that includes ample rest and time off. Schedule regular days off to recharge, even if it feels tempting to keep working during peak times. Consider setting monthly or quarterly goals that include breaks or lighter work periods, especially after particularly demanding weeks. This rhythm will help keep your energy levels up and prevent burnout.

Another way to ensure sustainability is by creating a "wind-down" routine at the end of each workday. This could be as simple as a few minutes of stretching, some time for a personal hobby, or a brief walk to signal the end of the workday. Having a consistent end-of-day habit can make it easier to mentally transition from work to home life, helping you fully rest and recharge.

Action Steps:

- Plan regular days off each week or month to maintain energy and prevent burnout.
- Set achievable monthly goals that include lighter work periods after busy weeks.
- Develop a post-work routine to signal the end of your workday and help you decompress.

By incorporating these health-focused habits into your daily routine, you'll be better equipped to handle the physical and mental demands of rideshare work. Keeping your well-being at the forefront ensures you can enjoy this career for the long haul, providing for your family while staying healthy and motivated.

5

Conclusion

As we wrap up, let's take a moment to revisit the journey we've covered together. In this book, you've learned practical strategies to build a profitable and balanced rideshare career, from getting prepared for your first shift to maximizing income, managing your schedule around family needs, and taking care of your health and well-being. Each chapter has focused on giving you the tools and confidence to navigate the gig economy with a clear sense of purpose.

Throughout this journey, we've highlighted key practices to help you succeed:

- **Essential Preparations**: You're equipped with the tools, apps, and financial planning basics that set you up for a smooth start.
- **Market Awareness and Route Optimization**: You know how to identify high-demand areas and peak hours, maximizing your time on the road.
- **Schedule and Income Management**: You've built strategies for setting income goals, budgeting for variable earnings,

and creating a sustainable, family-friendly schedule.

· **Health and Well-Being**: You're armed with practical tips for maintaining physical and mental health while balancing work and family life, ensuring a long-lasting career in gig work.

But most importantly, you've learned how to be intentional and adaptable. The gig economy is a unique path that demands resilience, flexibility, and self-motivation. By taking control of your schedule, earnings, and personal well-being, you're not just working—you're building a career that supports your family and aligns with your life goals.

Final Thoughts and Words of Encouragement

As you go forward, remember that every shift is a step toward your bigger goals. There will be challenges, but keep in mind the reason you're here: to create a life where you have both time for your family and the income to support them. Trust yourself, stay adaptable, and don't be afraid to adjust your strategies as you go. Every ride is an opportunity to learn, refine your approach, and improve your skills.

In the end, this work is about more than just driving. It's about providing for your family, showing up when it matters most, and building a life on your terms. I started this journey with 2 kids in elementary school. Whether this book was your introduction to rideshare work or a guide to refining your approach, know that you're capable of achieving your goals. Keep moving forward with confidence, and remember that you're not alone on this journey.

www.ingramcontent.com/pod-product-compliance
Lightning Source LLC
Chambersburg PA
CBHW070138230526
45472CB00004B/1591